JUST RUBBISH?

Recycling
PLASTIC

Joy Palmer

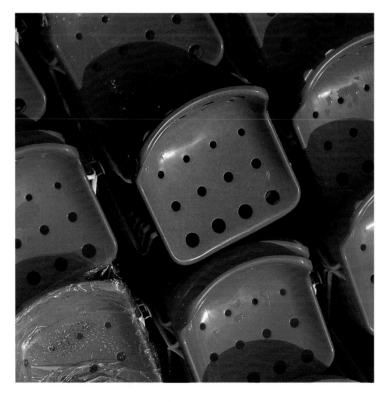

Franklin Watts

London/New York/Sydney/Toronto

CONTENTS

380110 55 12897 2

365.7

© 1990 Franklin Watts

First published in Great Britain in 1990 by
Franklin Watts
96 Leonard Street
London EC2A 4RH

First published in Australia by
Franklin Watts
14 Mars Road
Lane Cove
NSW 2066

Reprinted 1991, 1992

UK ISBN: 0 7496 0154 X

Printed in Belgium

Editor
Ruth Taylor

Picture researcher
Sarah Ridley

Designed by
Sally Boothroyd

Illustrations by
Jeremy Gower
Tony Kenyon
Raymond Turvey

Photographs
Ecoscene/Sally Morgan pages 14, 15; Eye Ubiquitous
9, 12, 16-17; Chris Fairclough Colour Library 5, 6-7,
10, 17; thanks to Joanne Fox 22; Robert Harding
Picture Library 13; courtesy of Isle of Wight County
Council 21; courtesy of North London Waste
Authority 20; courtesy of Safeway plc 23; Wagner
International 27.

Acknowledgment
The author and publishers thank Pippa Hyam, Senior
Information Officer, Friends of the Earth, for her
advice.

A CIP catalogue record for this book is
available from the British Library.

INTRODUCTION

Glance up from this page for a moment: almost certainly you will see plastic. Our homes, offices, schools, hospitals, factories – indeed, our entire surroundings – are dominated by products made from this material. We live in the age of plastics; bright, attractive, colourful, long-lasting, relatively inexpensive substances whose invention has revolutionized the manufacturing industry. Plastics certainly have advantages. Unfortunately, they also bring problems to our world, not the least among these being the generation of vast quantities of waste material.

This book is concerned with the complex question of dealing with plastic waste. There are dozens of different plastics in common use, and many products are made from a mixture of these, and so recycling is no simple or straightforward task. The process is complex for other reasons too – and cannot be understood in isolation from other key concepts associated with the behaviour and management of plastic waste products. The forthcoming pages introduce and discuss ideas such as source reduction of waste, precycling and degradability of plastics, which all inter-relate with the central issue of recycling. The book provides a comprehensive overview of the facts and issues involved, together with examples from around the world which demonstrate how progress is being made in effective waste management. It must be emphasized that plastic waste recycling and management are not merely the concern of large-scale schemes and companies. Every individual one of us can take action to deal effectively with plastic waste in our lives, and in this small way make an essential contribution towards improving our environment.

OUR PLASTIC AGE

In 1909 Leo Baekeland invented phenolics or Bakelite – a plastic material. Little would he have realized then what a profound effect this and other plastics would have upon ourselves and our earth. His invention marked the beginning of a new "plastic age" that has transformed many aspects of industry and our lives. Great enthusiasm greeted the discovery, and plastic was labelled the manufacturing material of the future. It proved to be clean, inexpensive, long-lasting, strong, and able to be produced in a wide range of bright and attractive colours.

The irony is that their strength and durability are two of the factors which make plastics cause serious disposal problems.

Currently, there are around 30 different types of plastic in regular use. Probably the easiest to identify is Polyethylene Terephthalate, or PET. It is used for the clear plastic bottles which we find in supermarkets, containing fizzy drinks such as lemonade and cola. PET soft drink bottles make up about 20 per cent of all moulded plastic containers. Seventy per cent are soft drink bottles made of another type of plastic, called high-density polyethylene or HDPE. Scrap from PET is used to make "fibre fill", a lining material for jackets, pillows and sleeping bags. It is also used as lining in the upholstery of furniture and as a fibre in the construction of carpets.

HDPE plastic is used in the manufacture of garden furniture, flower pots, toys, dustbins and various other sorts of plastic containers. Two further well-known plastics are polystyrene and polyvinyl chloride (PVC). PVC is commonly used for making records, margarine containers, coat hangers, food film and floor tiles.

We live in an age when plastics are taken for granted. The process of injection moulding has enabled everyday objects to be made with precision yet at low cost.

Millions of plastic products are manufactured each year throughout the world. As the technology for their production increases, even more products will enter the "plastic age". Many of the plastic products around you are made by a process known as injection moulding. Molten plastic is squirted into a mould, where it quickly cools and reproduces the shape and form of the mould itself. When the plastic has cooled, the mould is opened to reveal the finished product. This amazingly quick and accurate process is used for a variety of goods, from dustbins to high-precision watch parts, and including items such as kettles, irons and cookware. Almost no labour costs are involved, and therefore plastic products are inexpensive compared to those made from other materials. They are also colourful, attractive and easily cleaned. We are living in a plastic age, with its many advantages. Unfortunately, it is an age which brings inevitable and serious problems for our earth.

Plastic objects are ideal for the kitchen because they are easily cleaned. People also like them because they are bright and colourful.

New plastic objects are produced every day. Even racing cars can now be made out of plastics.

PROBLEMS WITH PLASTICS

Two of the virtues of plastics, their strength and their durability, are also what makes them problematic. Plastics are often used to manufacture products for which they are actually inappropriate: that is, strong and long-lasting plastics are used to make things that are almost immediately thrown away!

Most plastics are made of polymers, long, complex molecules that are derived originally from oil supplies. As the world's reserves of oil are dwindling, this obviously raises serious issues. It is estimated that, if we continue using oil at the present rate, then known reserves on the earth will be used up in only 30 years' time. Even allowing for the potential of yet undiscovered oil reserves, the world may run out of this important substance within 50 years. Any attempts at conservation are therefore vital.

Two examples of this misuse are shopping bags and food containers. We are all accustomed to packing away our groceries into plastic carrier bags. The plastic material in these bags will last for many years, and yet we often unpack and throw them away within a short time of acquiring them.

Plastic food containers are a similar example of the inappropriate use of materials. Many fast food restaurants serve food and hot drinks in polystyrene containers which are designed to keep their contents hot for the duration of the meal. The actual life of such a container is potentially hundreds of years … yet purchasers enjoy the contents, and then toss it into the nearest bin within minutes.

Plastic carrier bags from the supermarket and polystyrene containers for "fast food": two examples of long-lasting plastic put to short-lived use. This represents an unfair exchange of resources.

1950

Plastic

Paper

Ashes and cinders

The same is true of all plastic food wrapping and packaging: as soon as the goods are removed, plastic boxes, plastic bags, polystyrene containers and plastic film wrap all head for the waste bin.

To make this situation even worse, the discarded plastic could be in our world for limitless time. It is generally accepted that plastics are not biodegradable: that is, they cannot be broken down biologically into simpler substances (more about this on pages 12-13 and 16-17). Objects that we may use for a few minutes could remain in the world more or less forever.

This represents an unfair and problematic exchange of materials. Valuable and irreplaceable reserves of oil are being used up to make objects, such as hamburger containers and shopping bags, that are then used only briefly, but may litter our world for generations.

Certainly we are in the plastics age – an era of cheap and useful products that are so readily disposed of that they generate vast amounts of problematic waste. More and more plastic is being used in the world, and so its volume of waste is forever increasing. Because plastics are so light (think of bags, for example), their contribution to the weight of waste in the world is deceptively small. In the UK and the USA, for example, plastics make up only 7 per cent of the weight of household waste. By volume, however, they make up some 20-30 per cent of the total.

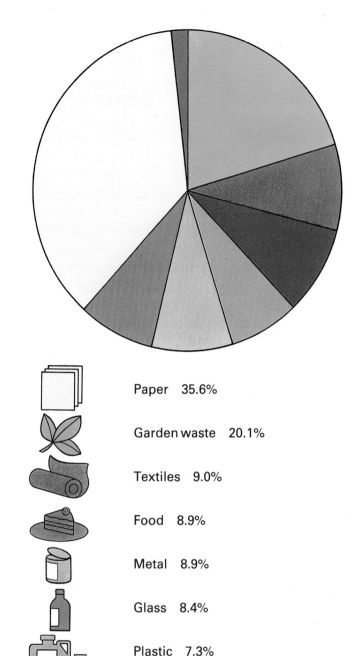

Paper 35.6%

Garden waste 20.1%

Textiles 9.0%

Food 8.9%

Metal 8.9%

Glass 8.4%

Plastic 7.3%

Miscellaneous 1.8%

Percentages by weight of different materials in household waste. (Figures from the United States Environmental Protection Agency.)

1990

Paper   Plastic   Ashes and cinders

The changing profile of waste. Household waste has changed dramatically in the past fifty years. There has been a steady decrease in ashes and cinders, and a great increase in paper and plastics.

PLASTIC WASTE

Increasing plastic use means increasing plastic waste. Many people are quick to point out that this ever-growing volume of waste from the plastic industry is no serious problem, since it can be buried or burned. This is true, but with far-reaching and controversial consequences. Some people argue that the incineration of plastic is hazardous, because poisonous gas is given off during the process. Other scientific studies conclude that when it is properly incinerated, plastic converts to carbon dioxide and water vapour, and that it is a non-toxic process.

Burying plastic waste is also a matter of controversy and concern. A great deal of the world's solid waste is disposed of by burying it in huge holes in the ground known as landfills. In Britain today, around 80 per cent of waste is buried in this way. The remainder is incinerated or recycled for further use. Plastics are certainly included in this 80 per cent figure and are often singled out for criticism because they are considered to be non-degradable – that is, they will not eventually rot away.

Another problem is that plastics buried underground are known to give off a poisonous gas. PVC gives off a gas called vinyl chloride. Even in our homes and workplaces it is possible to detect this gas in association with PVC. Studies in the United States of America have found tiny quantities of it in households and plastics factories. Indeed, it has been blamed as the cause of liver cancer in workers in the plastics industry. In burial sites for waste, much larger quantities of the gas have been identified and measured, raising serious concern to those living nearby.

Red and yellow plastics generally contain a poisonous substance called cadmium. If these plastics are degradable, it is likely that rain water will wash the cadmium from the landfill site and transfer it into our water supplies.

A scavenging horse at the Tirjohn landfill site, Swansea, Wales. Eighty per cent of solid waste in Britain is buried in huge holes in the ground called landfills. Plastics are included in this process. One problem is that the rubbish may contain toxins, which are washed out of the soil by rainwater. It is possible that these poisonous substances may pollute water supplies.

Smoke pours from the chimney of this incineration plant in Devon. This is obviously an environmental hazard. Not only does it look unsightly, but also it is polluting the atmosphere. The incineration of waste is a controversial process. Smoke may travel over long distances, carrying pollutants with it.

A final hazard related to gas from discarded plastics is associated with the problem of waste dumps accidentally catching fire. Smoke from burning PVC and polystyrene foams contains the gas hydrogen fluoride, which has an unpleasant smell and is very poisonous.

This whole question of plastic waste is complex and controversial. Those in favour of using waste as landfill argue that plastics have sound advantages: because they are unlikely to rot away, they actually give stability to the tip as a whole, making a solid and safe foundation so that the land, when filled in, may be reclaimed as a safe site for building and development.

Getting rid of plastics is therefore not easy. Some people argue that it makes more sense not to use them at all. Those involved with the plastics industry would obviously disagree, yet are concerned that care should be taken of the earth's resources and of the environment. Plastics have many environmental advantages: for example, it takes less energy to make products in plastics than in other materials; plastics are also lighter and easier to store and transport, leading to energy savings compared to other raw materials.

What is certain is that attention must be paid to more careful and sensible use of plastics and, perhaps more importantly, we must find ways of re-using or recycling them to good advantage.

toxins may be released from buried waste and washed into streams and rivers

solid waste is buried in landfills

THE RECYCLING PROCESS

These plastic bottles have been collected for recycling. They have been squashed and stacked in bales, ready to be reprocessed.

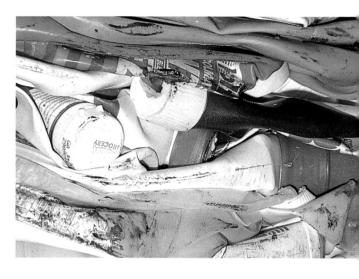

Despite the fact that developed and industrial nations are well into the plastic age, it is a relatively new industry. The concept of recycling, that is, putting materials to effective re-use, is also in the early phase of growth, research and development. A great deal of attention is currently being paid to this all over the world.

In Britain, for example, the British Plastics Federation is strongly committed to promoting research and encouraging the industry to develop the potential of plastics for recycling. A number of issues make this a complex task. Many of the measures that could be taken to promote recycling are expensive and complicated to organize and implement. Related to this is the fact that recycling of plastics is limited because it is difficult, and sometimes impossible, to identify and separate them according to their particular chemical type. All plastics may look alike, but chemically they differ widely and will react in different ways. Some, for example, can be melted down. Others will stay in solid form when heated, until a critical temperature is reached, when they will catch fire.

Coding systems are being devised for recycling. In the United States of America, the plastics industry has devised a voluntary system of coding containers so that recyclers can identify different types of plastic and separate them for efficient recycling. By 1990, 12 states had adopted this system and others were preparing for it.

The two kinds of plastic that can be easily identified and recycled are polyethylene terephthalate (PET) and high-density polyethylene (HDPE). In their original existence these are probably used to make containers of soft drinks. In recycled form, however, they cannot be used for drinks containers. This is because, in recycling, the plastics are melted down at low temperatures and may be contaminated with dangerous substances that are released in the process. It would therefore not be safe to use them for making containers for anything that humans will consume.

PET bottle

paper label

polyethylene base

aluminium top

polystyrene container

aluminium foil top

Multi-material objects like these make recycling a more difficult task.

In the recycling process, machines heat the waste and melt down those plastics that will do this, so that they are turned into a sticky substance. Roughly, this is around three quarters of the total household plastic waste. The small solid remains that have not melted may be added and mixed in, producing a recycled rough mixture that can be poured into moulds and turned into new products such as floor tiles, railway sleepers, and sewage pipes. This is excellent use of plastic waste, since the raw material for the new products costs nothing. Also, the energy required for making recycled plastic is a tiny fraction of that needed for making new plastic. Environmentally and economically, this makes good sense.

A major complication in recycling is that objects may be made of more than one material. A PET bottle, for example, may have an aluminium top, a paper label and a polyethylene base. PET cartons may be blended with other polymers. New developments in the industry aim to manufacture single-polymer items, in order to make recycling easier.

This baling machine is at a plastics sorting centre in Sheffield. It squashes or compresses the used bottles.

Many plastic objects are recycled, to become different objects.

Polypropylene bottle crates and car battery boxes may become drainage pipes. In Britain, 25,000 tonnes of polypropylene are recycled each year.

Polystyrene cassettes from photographic film may become flower pots.

Polyethylene kitchen film may become black refuse bags. In Britain, 50,000 tonnes of polyethylene film is recovered each year.

15

DO PLASTICS ROT AWAY?

At present, nearly all of the plastics in use are strong and chemically stable. This means that they are resistant to natural decay, and more or less indestructible. When buried, these oil-based plastics are not biodegradable – that is, they do not decompose or rot away as a result of being broken down biologically into simpler substances.

One of the current major areas of research and development in the plastics industry is the production of degradable plastics. Indeed, it is possible to make materials that have many of the qualities of traditional plastics, but which can be biologically broken down by bacteria in the same way as paper and food wastes. Rather than being derived from oil, biodegradable plastics are made by the fermentation of substances such as sugar and other natural carbohydrates. One firm in the USA has made a degradable plastic with the aid of bacteria found in canals. The bacteria thrive and multiply on a carbohydrate diet, producing a "biological plastic" which can be extracted, dried and sold. This is easily broken down at a later stage, by bacteria in the soil in which it is buried. It is estimated that a shopping bag made from plastic of this kind will disappear a year or so after burial.

However, this type of biological plastic is quite rare. More frequently, biodegradable bags are made from a plastic with a starch additive. This plastic is still oil-based, and so does not eliminate the problem of using up oil reserves.

Another way in which some plastics may be degraded is by exposure to the light of the sun. This process is known as photodegradation, or the deterioration of a material by sunlight. Plastics are made photodegradable by adding a chemical when they are being manufactured which alters their composition. Such additives initiate and accelerate sensitivity to light.

Degradable plastics are becoming widely available and are used in many countries. In the UK and the USA photodegradable plastic shopping bags are increasingly available. In

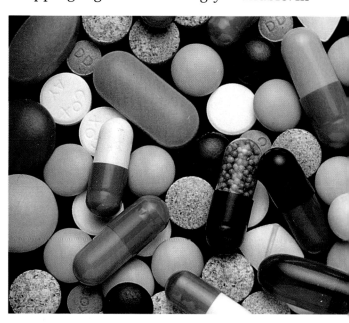

To some extent, plastics are broken down by sunlight. But once underground, they will not degrade at all.

After one year: the bottle looks much the same as it did on the day it was thrown away.

After five years: if exposed to sunlight, the bottle will partially decompose.

France, photodegradable plastics are turned into a mulch which is spread on the land. This helps keep moisture and warmth in the soil so that crops grow earlier in the year. Degradable plastics have also become useful to doctors and surgeons: for example, stitches after operations can be made of materials which dissolve into the body and do not have to be cut away.

Such developments are exciting, but not without controversy. Degradable plastics are far more expensive to produce than traditional, oil-derived ones. Additives like cadmium (see page 12) may leak into water sources. Also, the time that it takes for these "new" plastics to break down can only be estimated. Many factors affect the process, including temperature and moisture. Because their life span is not known, degradable plastics cannot be recycled. This complicates even further current attempts at sorting for recycling. Also, there is obviously a climatic problem associated with photodegradable items. A product made for a cool climate may not be serviceable in a warm, sunny land. It must be stressed that photodegradation is not going to solve the problem of solid waste disposal. Plastics of this kind that are placed in landfill sites and covered with soil will never disintegrate, because they will not be exposed to the necessary sunlight. Photodegradable bags are actually discounted by some environmentally aware organizations, because it is argued that they encourage people to throw them on the ground as litter.

On balance, it would seem that, because plastics are made from non-renewable resources, we should be concentrating efforts into recycling them, not altering them so that they degrade into the earth.

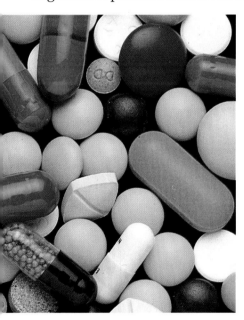

Degradable plastic is used for medicated capsules which release drugs into the human body at controlled rates.

Degradable plastic carrier bags sound a good idea. But do they encourage litter?

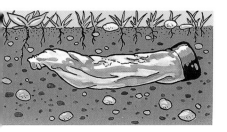

After twenty years: once buried, the bottle will remain intact indefinitely.

PRECYCLING AND SOURCE REDUCTION

There is no easy solution to the problems of waste plastics, and any management programme needs to take account of a number of possibilities. The promotion of recycling for future use is essential. Nevertheless, many would argue that there is a vital stage which comes before recycling, namely *pre*cycling.

This means encouraging people to buy goods packaged in biodegradable or recyclable materials. The word was used in a campaign in the city of Berkeley, California, which urged consumers to buy food in recyclable packaging. The campaign's sensible slogan was "Reduce waste *before* you buy!" This involves making correct buying choices. By precycling, we can prevent large amounts of inappropriate materials from getting into solid waste disposal systems. Each person in the USA uses around 190 pounds (86 kg) of plastic every year, and one third of this is packaging which is thrown away as soon as the goods are removed. It is estimated that if 10 per cent of Americans bought products with less plastic packaging, just 10 per cent of the time, the country could eliminate 144,000,000 pounds (65,000,000 kg) of plastic from landfill and reduce industrial pollution.

Linked to precycling is the important concept of source reduction. In simple terms, this means generating less waste from the start – designing, manufacturing and using products with the aim of reducing both the quantity and the toxicity of the world's waste. If there is no waste, there are no problems in disposing of it! Without doubt, reducing waste at its source is the most sensible way of tackling a complex problem, from both an environmental and an economic point of view. This is particularly true in our plastic age.

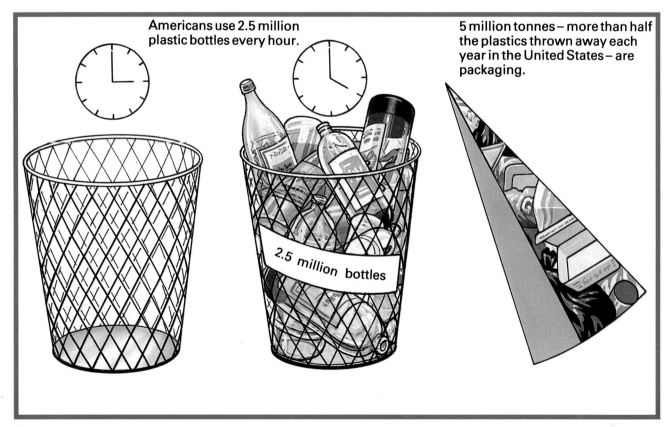

Americans use 2.5 million plastic bottles every hour.

2.5 million bottles

5 million tonnes – more than half the plastics thrown away each year in the United States – are packaging.

Source reduction is about sound management: those who manufacture goods and those who consume them are required to think about possible environmental costs and gains. It is linked to the idea of precycling, insofar as consumers must consider what they are buying and the likely effect on the environment – making positive choices, and reusing items when possible, rather than discarding them. From a manufacturer's point of view, it involves making items with fewer raw materials, producing goods that will last longer, and providing products that are easier to recycle.

Many of these issues have already been raised in relation to plastic. An excellent place to start reducing waste is with packaging: a high proportion of plastics produced are for packing items with life spans of a few hours. Some of this packaging serves a useful purpose and actually protects the product. Unfortunately, however, more often than not, it is merely to attract the buyer.

Everything you buy affects the environment in some way. Buy eggs in cardboard boxes, not plastic containers. Buy vegetables loose, not in plastic wrapping.

An equation for the environment: PRECYCLE + RECYCLE = REDUCED WASTE. You are precycling if you choose glass bottles rather than plastic bottles, because you know glass bottles can be recycled.

FROM PET TO PANTS –

The word recycling immediately brings to mind the reuse of materials to manufacture *new* products, and indeed this is a key aspect of it. In Yorkshire, England, for instance, reclaimed PET drinks bottles are being used to make trousers! Polymer Technologies developed a system for PET reclamation, and supplies two clothing companies with recycled material that can be turned into fibre, then woven into cloth to make trousers and anoraks. One tonne of reclaimed material mixed with a tiny amount of new polyester is enough to make 2,000 pairs of trousers: in other words, one pair of trousers needs only ten PET bottles. This example represents an important development in recycling, namely the acceptance of PET for use in fibre for clothing. The cost is approximately half that of using new polymer.

Further developments must be related to the quality of recycled PET. Research continues into how recycled PET could be made safe for food and drink containers. However, even if the recycling process can be refined so that consistent and pure PET is available, the cost of this may prove to be a deterrent. Also, public opinion cannot be ignored. Where something as important as the cleanliness and purity of food and drinks containers is concerned, adverse publicity may cause recycling in the food packaging industry to fail.

Solid waste is used for fuel at this power station in Edmonton, North London. Steam from the waste incineration powers electricity generators.

Ten plastic bottles recycled provide material for one pair of trousers.

RECYCLING FOR ENERGY

Recovering actual material is not the only way to recycle plastics: it is also possible to recover their heat or thermal content, which provides a source of energy without using up new fuel. A typical assortment of household waste contains polymers which can be recovered through a process of controlled combustion, to provide heat and steam to generate electricity. A number of successful schemes employ this process, including one in Edmonton, North London, where an incinerator produces steam from solid waste to power electricity generation. The electricity generated is sold to the Eastern Electricity Board.

Another way in which recycling plastics can help save traditional energy sources is that waste containing plastics can be reprocessed to make pellets of solid fuel. One example of a refuse-derived fuel plant in Britain is at Newport on the Isle of Wight. This establishment should produce 20,000 tonnes of refuse-derived fuel each year from 63,000 tonnes of waste. The process involves the manufacture of small and easy-to-store fuel pellets which are currently being used to heat one of the island's colleges and a school.

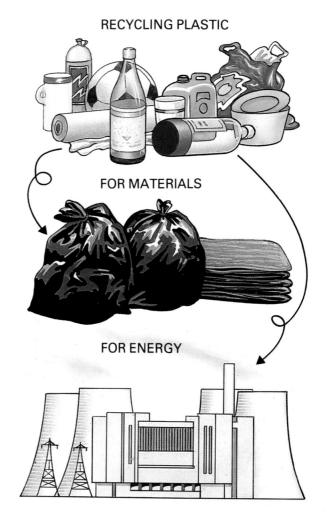

RECYCLING PLASTIC

FOR MATERIALS

FOR ENERGY

Recycling plastics has a double value: for new materials and for energy.

Refuse-derived fuel pellets made at the Isle of Wight plant.

WHERE THE ACTION IS: THEY RECYCLE

Around the world there are many examples of schemes and initiatives which recycle plastics successfully. In May 1989, Sheffield became known as Britain's first "Recycling City", when a major campaign to put waste to good use was launched by Friends of the Earth. As part of this initiative, the British Soft Drinks Association and the British Plastics Federation agreed to sponsor 25 plastic-bottle banks in the city. The scheme, now managed by the British Plastics Federation, welcomes all kinds of plastic bottles: opaque (non-clear) ones, such as those for washing-up liquids, washing machine detergents, fabric softeners, and toiletries, as well as others for fresh fruit juice and milk, and transparent (clear) ones, such as those that have contained fizzy drinks and mineral water. Consumers are asked to deposit these in one of the coloured collection banks which are emptied regularly by a local contractor (a local firm employed for this task). Plastic-bottle banks are very rare in the UK. Other cities taking initiatives include Leeds, with its "Bertie Bottle" collection scheme, and Cardiff, which became the second "Recycling City" in May 1990. However, other places are set to become sites of co-ordinated, large-scale recycling.

One of the aims of the whole "Recycling City" campaign is to study the cost-effectiveness of large-scale recycling schemes. Clearly, enough waste has to be collected to make the recycling process economically viable. This relates to an interesting news item from the United States, where PET recycling has become so successful in some manufacturing industries that there is actually a shortage of waste. The US National Association for Plastic Container Recovery is encouraging voluntary collection schemes, as well as counting on mandatory recycling laws which already apply to industries in some states. Indeed, kerbside and community recycling schemes are seen to be essential to the future of the US plastics industry.

All plastic bottles may be saved and recycled – coloured and transparent ones.

Saving banks for plastic bottles are often colour-coded for convenience. This yellow one in Sheffield is for coloured plastic bottles.

Well-known companies are certainly making headlines around the world in their attempts to promote successful recycling. Coca-Cola has joined with other organizations to create an efficient PET recycling scheme in Switzerland. This involves the establishment of collection points in sports areas, and the development of return-bottle schemes in supermarkets.

The Mobil Corporation is building the first commercial plastic-foam recycling plant in the USA, in Leominster, Massachusetts. Initially, this is designed to recycle polystyrene foam products and plastic cutlery used in school dining rooms and industrial cafeterias. Hopefully, the scheme will be expanded to include plastics from fast-food stores. A similar joint scheme by McDonald's Restaurants and the Amoco Corporation in New York City also aims to recycle foam plastics and plastic cutlery.

In a nationwide US programme, Browning-Ferris Industries, one of the largest haulers of solid waste, and the Wellman Corporation, the world's largest recycler of rigid plastic material, are combining in an effort to remove rigid plastic waste from the municipal solid waste stream and effectively recycle it.

Safeway foodstores set a good example with a scheme for recycling plastic carrier bags.

CODE FOR BOTTLE SAVERS:

Plastic bottle banks do not want glass bottles.

Please remove bottle caps.

Please rinse bottles.

WHERE THE ACTION CAN BE: YOU RECYCLE

Large companies and city-wide communities can obviously make a substantial impact with large-scale recycling schemes. However, the importance of the role of every individual person cannot be overestimated. Environmental action concerns each one of us, whether we contribute to a large community scheme or as an individual consumer. Residents of the City of Sheffield have a ready-made opportunity to recycle plastic waste with a minimum of effort, BUT a lot can be achieved by people who do not have this advantage.

Action...Action...Action... How to reduce plastic waste

★ If possible, refuse plastic containers for fast food. These are not essential, and often have a useful life of a few minutes only. Many purchases of this kind could be put into your own paper bag.

★ Refuse plastic bags in supermarkets. Take your own "environmentally friendly" shopping bag or ask your supermarket manager to provide paper bags.

★ Avoid disposable plastic at home. So much plastic is put to inappropriate use, for example, throwaway film and food bags. Instead of these, try using plastic food boxes, that will serve for a much longer time.

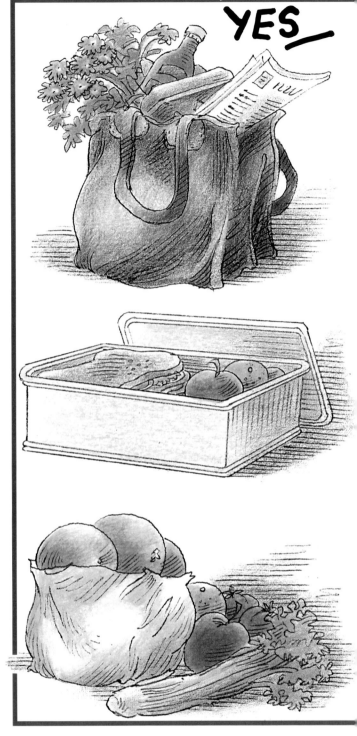

ACTION! WHAT YOU CAN DO
Use your own environmentally friendly shopping bag, rather than taking a plastic bag from the supermarket.

Use plastic containers that can be re-used, rather than plastic bags and cling film, when you make your packed lunch.

Choose unwrapped fresh foods, rather than the same foods wrapped in lots of plastic.

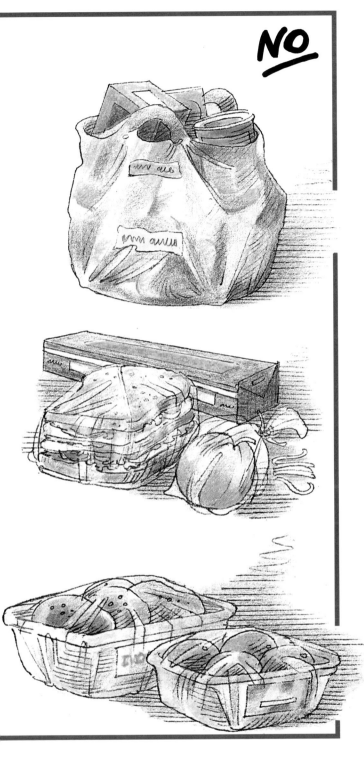

★ Select natural materials for clothes wherever possible. Try to avoid man-made fibres in clothing. Often plastic is disguised as leather in belts and shoes.

★ Avoid plastic packaging on fresh food. Quite often, especially in supermarkets, fresh foods are over-packaged: three potatoes, for example, may be placed on a plastic tray and then covered with plastic film. Goods such as potatoes, carrots, tomatoes and, indeed, all fresh fruits and vegetables can be purchased without this unnecessary wrapping and taken home in your own shopping bags.

This action is about SOURCE REDUCTION and PRECYCLING. Where it is possible to link this to organized RECYCLING schemes, so much the better.

Action Fact...
One out of every $11 spent on food in the USA goes to pay for packaging.

Action Fact...
30 per cent by weight of all plastics produced are used for packaging.

Action Fact...
Waste packaging accounts for one third by weight of all the waste in landfills.

Action Fact...
Around half, by weight, of all plastics we throw away every day is packaging.

Action Conclusion
SOURCE REDUCTION + PRECYCLING + RECYCLING = LESS WASTE, LESS POLLUTION

= A BETTER WORLD

CONCLUSIONS

Probably the two most important messages of this book are, first, that plastic recycling cannot be considered in isolation from other fundamental issues relating to the behaviour and management of waste products and, second, that dealing with waste is not the sole preserve of large schemes and companies. Every one of us can take a share in the action and achieve worthwhile results.

Key ideas and concepts have been discussed, namely, the nature and behaviour of plastics and their waste, bio- and photodegradation, the importance of source reduction, precycling and recycling. All of these are inter-related. In conclusion it must be emphasized that there is no single way forward in order to deal effectively with waste plastics and their potential problems. It is essential that nations throughout the world adopt an integrated waste management system – one that takes account of various possibilities, including source reduction, recycling, incineration and landfilling.

The US National Polystyrene Recycling Company recycles used food containers to make pellets of polystyrene. These can be made into office supplies, plastic trays, videotape holders and foam insulation.

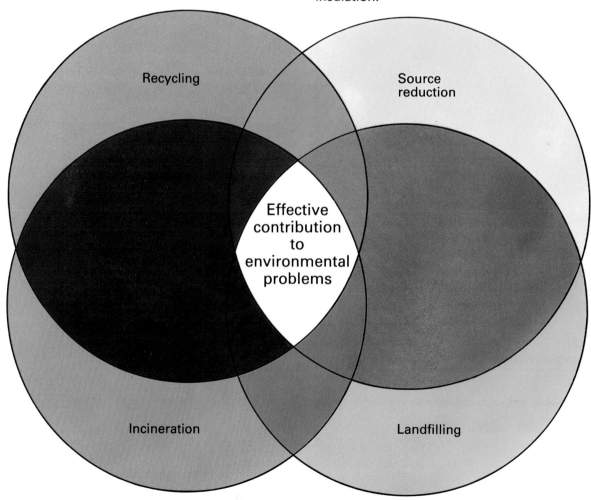

An integrated plastic waste management system is essential.

Having said that, probably the single most important development must be recycling. Because the vast majority of plastics are made from non-renewable vital resources, such as oil, every effort should be concentrated on putting them to good and repeated use rather than on disposing of them or modifying them so that they degrade into the environment.

The plastics industry is expanding rapidly, and with this growth is an associated surge of research into and development of recycling possibilities and techniques. It is good to know that international companies such as Mobil will continue to work on the technology for degradation and guarantee to provide degradable plastic products for customers who ask for them. Nevertheless, this alone will not provide a comprehensive solution to the world's solid waste problem. Much more needs to be done to promote recycling, as this clearly underpins any

effective solution. Fortunately, the plastics industry is well aware of this and is taking appropriate action.

Again to cite Mobil, this company and seven other polystyrene manufacturers have formed the National Polystyrene Recycling Company in the USA. NPRC's aim is to recycle one quarter of all disposable polystyrene products by 1995. Initiatives such as the City of Sheffield scheme are becoming increasingly common in the developed world, so that every one of us can readily participate in useful recycling action. As well as taking individual initiatives in source reduction and precycling, we can all encourage our local communities to adopt such measures and to consider larger-scale schemes. With combined action from industry and individuals, a great deal can be achieved in terms of making plastic a useful rather than a problematic addition to our world.

GLOSSARY

biodegradable can be broken down biologically into simpler substances.

combustion burning, consumption by fire.

decomposition breakdown of dead animal and plant life into simpler substances.

finite resources resources available in a limited supply, for example, coal and oil. One day we may use them all up.

molecule smallest particle or atom of which material substances consist.

photodegradable can be broken down by exposure to sunlight.

pollute to make dirty, foul or unclean.

polymers long, complex molecules derived from oil, and which are the component forms of plastics.

recycling the conversion of waste into a re-usable product.

source reduction reducing the amount of waste material generated.

waste that which is left over after use, superfluous, no longer serving a purpose.

ADDRESSES

British Plastics Federation, 5 Belgrave Square, London SW1X 8PD

British Soft Drinks Association Ltd, 6 Catherine Street, London WC2B 5UA

Community Recycling Opportunities Programme, 7 Burner's Lane, Kiln Farm, Milton Keynes MK11 3HA

Friends of the Earth, 26/28 Underwood Street, London N1 7JQ

Pennsylvania Resources Council, 25 West 3rd Street, Media, Pennsylvania 19063, USA

Solid Waste Management Solutions, Mobil Chemical Company, 1159 Pittsford-Victor Road, Pittsford, New York 14531, USA

Tidy Britain Group, publications available from The Pier, Wigan WN3 4EX

Warmer Campaign, 83 Mount Ephraim, Tunbridge Wells, Kent TN4 8BR

Waste Watch, 26 Bedford Square, London WC1B 3HU

RESOURCES

For further reading and information (send a stamped, addressed envelope for details of costs).

1) *Waste Issues* published by the Tidy Britain Group

2) Factsheets published by the British Plastics Federation

3) *The Environmental Shopper* (a list of US products that use recycled packaging, plus information booklet at $2)
Pennsylvania Resources Council

4) *Dustbin Power*, the Warmer Campaign

5) *The Dustbin Pack*, teacher's file, from Waste Watch

6) *Recycling* poster, available from Pictorial Charts Educational Trust, 27 Kirchen Road, London W13 0UD

In Australia, further information can be obtained from the following agencies in each capital city:

Environmental Protection Agency
Keep Australia Beautiful
Total Environment Centre
Waste Management Authority
or Your Local Council

INDEX